YOUR PARENTS' LOVE

Abbie Mabary

Your Parents' Love

Copyright © 2020 Abbie Mabary

Published by Lucid Books in Houston, TX.
www.LucidBooksPublishing.com

All rights reserved. No part of this publication may be reproduced, stored in a retrieval system, or transmitted in any form by any means, electronic, mechanical, photocopy, recording, or otherwise, without the prior permission of the publisher, except as provided for by USA copyright law.

ISBN-13: 978-1-63296-498-4
eISBN-13: 978-1-63296-888-3

Special Sales: Most Lucid Books titles are available in special quantity discounts. Custom imprinting or excerpting can also be done to fit special needs. Contact Lucid Books at info@lucidbooksPublishing.com

Dedicated to my children for welcoming all our bonus kiddos with open arms. The way you have loved your foster siblings has been a beautiful thing to witness. Thank you for riding this roller coaster with your dad and me.

The biggest thanks to my husband for your unwavering support of this book as well as all the dreams I have had over the years. You are truly my favorite.

Your parents love you so much.

They love to sing songs with you.

And read books to you.

And color pictures with you.

Your parents heard about a kid
who needs a safe place
to stay for a little while.

For one reason or another,
that kid's parents
aren't able to care for them.

Since your mom and dad really love being parents, they figured they could help this kid out for a while.

Someday soon, this kid might come to stay with your family.

When that kid comes to stay with you, they might feel sad or angry because they miss their first family.

And that's okay.

When they feel sad, it might be fun to sing songs

or play games

or read books

or color pictures with them.

And when they leave your family to go home to their first family, you might feel sad or angry.

And that's okay.

When you feel sad, you might ask your parents if they would like to sing a song with you.

Or play a game with you.

Or read a book to you.

Or color with you.

Your parents love you so much.

www.ingramcontent.com/pod-product-compliance
Lightning Source LLC
LaVergne TN
LVHW070948070426
835507LV00028B/3455